The Romans introduced the engagement ring as a sign of possession. However, the wedding ring is a symbol of harmony and unity.

❀ ❀

The Greeks considered that the third finger on the left hand was connected by a vein to the heart; hence, it is the common ring finger.

THE QUINTESSENTIAL WEDDING GUIDE

Maid of Honor

BY HEIDI L. HOLMES

Holmes, Heidi L.
The Quintessential Wedding Guide
Maid of Honor / By Heidi L. Holmes ("Author")
http://www.blueinkdesigns.com

ISBN 978-0-9805263-1-8

Published by Holmes Futures PL, Australia ("Publisher")
http://www.holmesfutures.com

 4

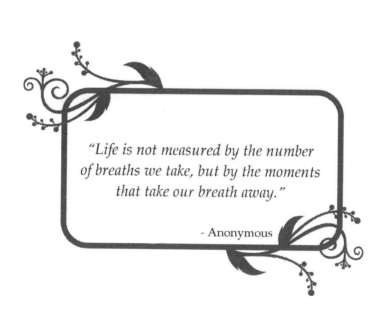

"Life is not measured by the number of breaths we take, but by the moments that take our breath away."

- Anonymous

TABLE OF CONTENTS

Introduction

❀ ❀

Chapter One

Chapter Two

Chapter Three

Chapter Four

Chapter Five

"Life is the flower for which love is the honey."

— Victor Hugo

Introduction

THE OFFICIAL OBLIGATIONS OF THE MAID OF HONOR

Congratulations! You have been asked to be the maid of honor at a wedding, and you are likely to be feeling a lot of different emotions. You must be excited and touched by this gesture of affection and trust from the bride.

Whatever your feelings are, lurking beneath the rush of emotions, there is undoubtedly a faint ripple of panic because you are not sure what this newly bestowed honor means.

What exactly are the duties of a maid or matron of honor? (Maid of honor if you are unmarried, matron of honor if you are.)

This book was written to be your guide and to help you become the most fabulous maid of honor ever!

Chapter by chapter, it will lead you through your obligations so you can fulfill them with elegance and humor.

Not only that, this book will make the process easy and fun. Because that is what being in a wedding party is all about, having fun!

Think of your new role as maid or matron of honor as the bride's helper, confidant, and closest friend. But more than anything, a maid of honor is an invaluable person because she connects the past and future of the bride. You hold the bride's most precious and most humorous memories, and you share her hopes and dreams for the future she is embarking upon.

You know her style well enough to know how she likes to party and what she craves for relaxation. You know her secret wild or shy side and how to keep her calm and grounded. In fact, you know enough to keep her wedding flowing smoothly and her parties in full swing!

Being a maid of honor requires a serious commitment to your friendship with the bride. It also demands smooth social skills and lots of energy. This book will not only inspire you as you prepare with the bride for the big day, but it will also save you time and spare you anxiety by spelling out exactly what your obligations are and how to fulfill them with flair, style, and grace.

You will find helpful information about being the most efficient contact person for the guests and the other bridesmaids, what exactly your duties are at the rehearsal dinner and at the wedding, and wonderful, creative suggestions for hosting a bridal shower and a bachelorette party.

You will find practical advice about managing the bridal registry plus suggestions for giving useful yet fabulous gifts. To your great relief, you will find a chapter that will offer suggestions for the maid of honor's toasts at all functions, including the rehearsal dinner and the wedding reception.

You will also find advice about how to be the maid of honor the bride is depending on while maintaining and expanding your friendship with her.

Most of all, this book will clarify what it means to be a maid of honor, from being a true friend to knowing when to offer a cocktail or two to the frazzled bride!

Chapter by chapter, this book will inspire both your laughter and your tears, while showing you how to party with creativity and class.

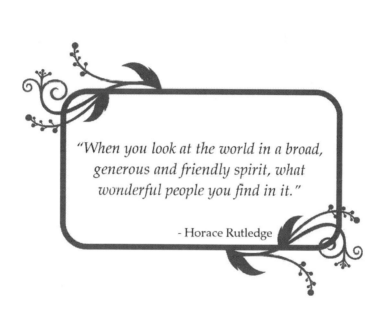

"When you look at the world in a broad,
generous and friendly spirit, what
wonderful people you find in it."

- Horace Rutledge

Chapter One

YOUR OBLIGATIONS AS THE CONTACT PERSON

The maid or matron of honor has a number of significant responsibilities. One of your most important duties is to be the central contact person for the guests and for the other bridesmaids.

What this means is that you need to gather all pertinent information regarding just about everything to do with the wedding and the pre-wedding events.

Not only do you need to know the dates and times of all wedding-related events, you need to try to find out about the bridal registry as well. If this comes down to poking through the bride's kitchen cabinets, well, that is what friends are for!

The Guests

It is very likely that wedding guests will be calling you with all kinds of unique and wonderful questions rather than bother the bride or groom.

To make things as easy for the bride as possible, get the complete guest list from her and begin contacting guests in order to introduce yourself and give out your contact information. Make sure to have important information handy, such as the date and time of the rehearsal dinner, the wedding shower, bachelorette party, the wedding ceremony, and the reception.

Also, do some research to locate nearby hotels. Be prepared with various transportation advice and offer to make both travel and hotel arrangements when needed for out-of-town guests. Find out every place that the bride and groom have registered for gifts.

If possible, arrange to get copies of the stores' registries and offer to send them to guests who are interested.

At the very least, get the name, location, and phone number of the bridal registry department of each store.

Do not be surprised if you get questions about whether the bride and groom prefer cappuccinos or lattes, or if they have a silver tea set! When guests call, encourage them to buy gifts for the bride and groom from their wedding registry.

THE BRIDESMAIDS

It is your role as maid of honor and good friend of the bride to coordinate all the other bridesmaids. You must make sure that everyone knows what she is supposed to do and where she is supposed to go, and then you must make sure everyone actually shows up in their dress wearing the correct heels! (On the correct day.)

Keep on top of exactly when the bridesmaids need to arrive at each event and then call the day before to remind them. Make sure you stay in touch with all out-of-town bridesmaids and help them arrange their travel and hotel reservations.

Use e-mail to make initial contact with the other bridesmaids, introducing yourself and supplying your address and phone number. Then follow up with phone calls. Ask all the bridesmaids to send you their e-mail and postal addresses.

Compile a list and send it to each bridesmaid, encouraging her to stay in touch with one another.

Maybe share something that you know about the bride, such as a humorous story or poignant memory to keep everyone focused on why you are all involved together (or have a good laugh at some old photographs).

Put together a written list of times, dates, and places that the bridesmaids are required to appear. Consider printing it out on beautiful paper to serve as a memento. Written information will be particularly helpful for any bridesmaids who are flying in from other states or cities.

Though it is traditional for the bride to choose bridesmaids' dresses that will complement her wedding colors, the best offer a maid of honor can make is to research bridesmaid dress designs so the bride doesn't have to.

Ask her about her general preferences, such as pastels, black and white, a specific color, style, or length. Start a dialogue with the other bridesmaids about size and style and relay any preferences to the bride.

Ultimately, the style of the bridesmaids' dresses is the bride's to choose, but you might remind her that one bridesmaid is six feet tall and a size eight while another bridesmaid is only five feet tall and a size fourteen.

Try to make tactful suggestions to help the bride find a bridesmaid's dress that will flatter all the bridesmaids in her wedding party. (This may mean suggesting the same color but different style of dress for each bridesmaid.)

It is your job as maid of honor to make sure that all the bridesmaids' dresses are properly ordered and that they arrive in time for alterations. You should also be prepared to pay for your own dress, shoes, and alterations.

Track down exactly how much the dress will cost, assemble several different choices for shoes, and find out about the cost for alterations. Then e-mail this information to all the bridesmaids well in advance of actually ordering any dresses.

If any bridesmaid has difficulty coming up with the necessary funds, act as a messenger between her and the bride. Sometimes brides will offer to help with the cost of bridesmaids' dresses.

Sit down with the bride and figure out a way to help out any bridesmaid who cannot afford her wedding attire.

Use this period to make friends among the bridesmaids. You might find some help when it comes to planning the wedding shower and bachelorette party!

The Rehearsal Dinner

The rehearsal dinner is traditionally held the night before the wedding at the place where the wedding ceremony will be performed. Sometimes the ceremony is rehearsed first, and then the dinner is held in another location.

Be on hand to help the bride plan her rehearsal dinner, and if she wants to have a sit-down dinner after the ceremony is rehearsed, be prepared to offer suggestions. It is a good idea to buy pre-printed wedding rehearsal invitations and send them out to all the bridesmaids and other invited guests at least three weeks before the rehearsal dinner. Make sure to include precise directions to the location for the ceremony and dinner for those who are unfamiliar with the area.

The entire wedding party, the bride and her fiancé's immediate families, the officiate and spouse, as well as out-of-town guests are traditionally included in the guest list.

Family and friends of the bride or the host may also be invited. It is also appropriate to invite the spouse or significant other of each attendant.

Contact all of the bridesmaids well in advance of the rehearsal dinner date and make sure they can all attend. If anyone has a problem, discuss it with the bride and see if another date and time can be arranged. It will be your job to make sure all the bridesmaids know where the rehearsal dinner will be held and what time they must arrive. Make sure to check with all out-of-town bridesmaids the week before and help with any last-minute travel and hotel arrangements. Then call everyone the day before and confirm the rehearsal dinner information and arrival time.

The rehearsal dinner is the perfect time to introduce yourself to everyone involved in the wedding. Make sure you have a good idea who everyone is and how he or she is related to the bride and groom before the night of the rehearsal dinner.

The rehearsal dinner is the best opportunity for you to ensure the bridesmaids are prepared for the following day (it may also be the first time of actually seeing people face-to-face). It is your job to help them with their dresses, see that they are where they should be, and guide them through the ceremony. It is also a good time to make sure everyone is relaxed and confident.

When dinner is served, there is usually a series of toasts. Either the father of the groom or the person who is hosting the dinner usually gives the first toast. The father of the bride usually follows with his own toast. Next, the best man makes a toast, followed by the maid of honor and any members of the wedding party who feel moved to join in.

Finally, the bride and groom make toasts.

As maid of honor, you should compose your toast well before the rehearsal dinner and practice it until you feel comfortable. Do not hesitate to make up small note cards to prompt you if your mind suddenly goes blank.

Try not to read your toast as this may spoil the lighthearted mood of a rehearsal dinner. Your toast should sound natural and from the heart. Do not be afraid to add sudden inspirational thoughts when the time comes to actually stand up and make your toast.

When composing a toast, there are several guidelines that you should keep in mind. Your toast should sound sincere and honest. Do not try to make a presidential speech! Speak from your heart and avoid clichés. Using any personal anecdotes about your long friendship with the bride is always a good idea. If you have not known the bride that long, consider talking to her mother to discover any insider information that you can incorporate into your toast.

Do avoid off-color remarks, references to any ex-spouses, any type of profanity, or any depressing subjects. Your toast should be upbeat and affectionate. This is not the time to offer condolences for the recent death of your best friend's hamster!

Before your toast, watch your alcohol consumption. The last thing you want to come out of your mouth is a slurred speech. When it is time to deliver your toast, stand and hold your glass up to get everyone's attention. Wait until the party is mostly silent.

Once you begin your toast, everyone will probably quiet down to listen. Make sure you speak clearly and loudly enough for everyone to hear. Maintain eye contact with the bride and groom throughout your toast and smile often. Consciously try to relax. Avoid nervous behavior, such as fiddling with your hair, shuffling your feet, holding your hand in front of your mouth, picking at your clothing, tapping your feet, or fidgeting in general.

Also avoid common speech ticks, such as "Umm," and "I mean," and "It's like." Don't talk too fast, no matter how much you want to get the toast over with! If you find your speech is running away with itself, take a deep breath and slow down!

Last of all, keep the pitch of your voice deep in your chest rather than letting it rise to a high squeak. Modulate your tone so that it varies throughout your toast.

You are not trying to put the wedding party to sleep after all! The following is a general outline for a short maid of honor's toast to the bride; however, in chapter nine you will find additional toast samples:

I would now be honored to propose a toast to (name of the bride). You have been the most loving, understanding, supportive friend anyone could ever hope to have. I have never met anyone with more compassion than you, or anyone who listens with all her heart to her friends and family.

Thank you for being like a sister to me, and I wish you a beautiful, fruitful life with (name of the groom). No one deserves happiness more than the two of you. To my closest, dearest friend, (name of the bride).

After the rehearsal dinner, make sure that all the bridesmaids have proper transportation and remind them of when and where they have to be throughout the actual wedding day.

"A Hug is the perfect gift.
One size fits all and nobody
minds if you exchange it."

- Anonymous

Chapter Two

OBLIGATIONS BEFORE THE WEDDING

One of the main aims of the maid of honor is to try to ensure that the wedding runs smoothly and is an enjoyable, memorable occasion. Your obligations then begin in the planning stage when you should assist the bride with many of the decisions and arrangements she must make.

Try to be as generous with your time and energy as possible. The bride is relying on you to be there for her!

WEDDING VENUES

Finding the perfect place for the ceremony and the reception is one of the essential elements that dictates the overall success of a wedding. Because the location is such an important factor and such an enormous expense, there is a lot of stress associated with making this decision.

As maid of honor, offer to go along with the bride to scout different wedding venues. Keep in mind that, these days, there is a large variety of unconventional places to have both the ceremony and reception. For example, consider the following locations:

- Historic Estates
- Castles
- Museums
- Art Galleries
- Public Gardens
- Yachts
- Beaches

❧ Country Inns

❧ Luxury Hotels

❧ Concert Halls

❧ Waterfront Restaurants

❧ Theaters

Of course, there are traditional party spaces, which will probably be less expensive since they are in the business of hosting events. However, remember that the location of the wedding is extremely important to setting the atmosphere. As a friend who knows the bride on a deep, personal level, you are in the perfect position to make suggestions based on what you know about the unique qualities, history, and style of the bride.

Begin by sitting down and having a thorough brainstorming session with the bride. Once you have an idea of her preferences, offer to make phone calls and arrange times to go and look at spaces.

Get the bride's schedule first and be sure to consult her before you make any appointments. Don't forget to consider the season when suggesting locations. Outdoor weddings always carry the risk of bad weather, which can add more stress to the bride.

If the bride is set on having her wedding in the nearby rose gardens, suggest arranging for tents or a backup site in case there is a rain shower on the day of the wedding. (It's a good idea to have a couple of umbrellas in the back of your car.)

Choosing Invitations

Planning a wedding is filled with countless small details, all of which should blend together to create a harmonious experience. One of the tone-setters for the wedding is the look of the invitations.

As maid of honor, you can help the bride choose the invitations and then assist in the mailing if she decides to do it herself.

The wedding industry is vast and profitable. As a result, the mailing of invitations may be a costly expense, so your focus should be on helping the bride make sure her money is spent wisely.

The design of the invitations is the first hint the guests will receive as to the style and theme of the wedding. They should reflect the formal, elegant, casual, or wacky style that the bride is aiming for in her planning.

One of the easiest ways to begin this process is to go with the bride to a printer or stationery store where they have large invitation catalogs. These catalogs contain examples of paper stock, color, typeface, and wording. Some of these invitations have preprinted text, and some are blank for your own choice of words.

There are also a lot of small designers whose business is based on creating unique, personal invitations, or perhaps you wish to consider a poem written for the occasion. These designers and printers can be more expensive than the big invitation manufacturers, so it depends on how unique the bride wants her invitations to be.

Go through the local phone directory and a local newspaper and accumulate a list of potential printers.

You might sit down and help the bride formulate the exact wording of her invitations first and also toss around a few ideas in terms of style and cost.

Remember that invitations consist of several parts including envelopes, RSVP cards and their envelopes, and reception cards.

Aim to help the bride send out her invitations at least eight weeks before the date of the wedding. Remind the bride to request her RSVPs at least three weeks in advance so she knows how many people will attend.

Decorations and Favors

Ask the bride if she needs any help in choosing and ordering both decorations and wedding favors. Even though she may want to keep the final wedding favors as a surprise, your input early on will probably help.

You should also take on the task of making sure that all decorations arrive on time for the bridal shower, the bachelorette party, and the actual wedding.

Get a list of suppliers that the bride has chosen and reassure her you will take over once she has made her choices.

Of course, you will be responsible on your own for choosing and ordering the decorations for the bridal shower and bachelorette party, but there will be more about that in later chapters of this book.

Seating Arrangements

Once the bride and groom and their families have determined the guest list and invitations have been sent out, it is time to figure out the seating arrangements. Considering the possible consequences of placing the wrong people next to each other, planning the scating arrangements is not only stressful, it's also difficult.

Not only that, it's probably one of the least fun tasks to which the bride must attend. As her good friend and maid of honor, offer to help the bride map out the seating. Obviously, the more guests who are coming, the harder this job will be.

One of the best ways of getting this task done is to come prepared with a large piece of paper, plenty of pencils, and a few good erasers. Then, draw out the number of tables and circles for corresponding chairs and, with guest list in hand, start writing in names.

You might have the bride write down, next to each guest's name on a list, whom they should not be seated next to.

Reassure the bride that it is impossible to make everyone happy. Keep moving people around until you come up with most perfect arrangement as possible. Once you have the plan set, offer to make a few copies.

Make sure one copy gets to the staff at the reception site so they can set up place cards. It is also a good idea to bring an extra copy yourself to the wedding in case things get mixed-up.

REGISTERING FOR GIFTS

This is the fun part! Registering for gifts gives the bride little bursts of time to relax and dream.

In the event that the groom is not available to go with her, don't miss the opportunity to have a great time and help the bride. Offer to go to the stores with her to register for wedding gifts.

Suggest that the bride register in both large department stores and smaller specialty stores; this will make it easier for guests who are not local. Plan to look at gifts at a relaxed pace; help the bride choose colors, patterns, and exact model numbers. Your shopping trips should be as fun and easygoing as you can make them (after all you are SHOPPING). A gift registry is ultimately about getting some really lovely wedding gifts that will act as mementos when the wedding day has passed. Try to remind the bride to slow down and relax and enjoy the experience.

Be sure to get a copy of the gift registry for every store at which the bride and groom are registered. If you can, find out each store's policy on returns and exchanges and keep records of every store's policy.

Finally, as maid of honor, offer to take on the task of letting all the guests know exactly where the bride and groom are registered. Either fax, mail, or e-mail her guests the name, phone number, and address of every store.

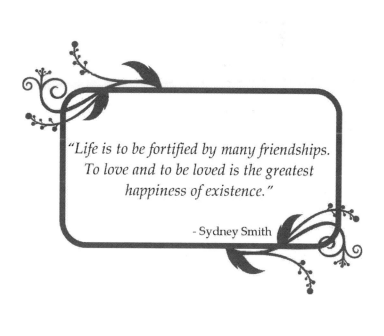

"Life is to be fortified by many friendships. To love and to be loved is the greatest happiness of existence."

- Sydney Smith

Chapter Three

THE DRESSES

As maid of honor, you may actually have some input into choosing the bridesmaids' dresses, shoes, and accessories. You are responsible for ordering the dresses and helping to arrange the fittings and alterations.

Then you must coordinate the time when each bridesmaid must show up for her fittings and make sure each bridesmaid obtains everything she needs to be ready for the big day.

However, the bride may choose the dresses without your input, and you should be graceful in accepting her decisions.

Additionally, you may be asked to help the bride shop for her own wedding dress.

THE BRIDE'S DRESS

It is a good idea for the bride to make appointments with several bridal salons to see what is available. Often, trying on a number of different styles will help her narrow down her definition of her "dream gown."

This is one area where the bride will greatly appreciate input from a source outside her family but still from someone who is very close to her. As maid of honor, you are perfect for the job!

It is extremely important that the shop the bride purchases her dress from has a good business record. With all the stresses surrounding a wedding, "The Dress" is one of the largest sources.

The bride needs to be assured that her dress will arrive on time and that the fittings will all be done in time for her wedding day.

You can help her out by researching the business history of the bridal shops she is interested in checking out. If you find any questionable history, recommend to the bride that she overlook those establishments.

Here is a checklist to have on hand regarding bridal shops. Make sure you gently remind the bride of these most important points.

Speak to the owner of the store and find out how long it has been in business. If possible, speak to one or more former customers and get the lowdown on their buying experience.

Ask about the price of alterations in advance, and if possible press to arrange a fixed rate on the completed dress (including undergarments, skirts, hidden corseting, etc.).

Find out the exact date when the store will order the bridal gown. Ask for written verification of the order, and offer to call the shop to check that the order has been placed.

Get everything involving the purchase of the wedding gown in writing. This includes the delivery date, the price of both the gown and alterations, and the store's policy if the gown is damaged.

Encourage the bride to start shopping around as soon as she sets her wedding date. The process of finding, ordering, and altering a wedding gown can take up to six months. The bride may want to take more than one person with her for input, so arrange to go on alternative days because too much input can be less helpful than no input at all.

Consider taking a camera with you when you go shopping with the bride for her dress. That way she can look at the dresses when she is at home and get many other opinions. However, be aware that many bridal shops will not allow you to take photos.

They do not want you comparison shopping, and they do not want their designs stolen by another store.

Still, it is always worth a try, so just slip a disposable camera in your purse and be sweet as sugar when asking if you can take photos.

Assure the salons they are for the bride and her family and friends only! Remain polite at all times, especially if they insist you leave your camera in the car.

As maid of honor, your role is simply to give feedback and suggest options. Once the bride has chosen her gown, she still has to coordinate and buy a veil, handbag, shoes, jewelry, and gloves.

THE BRIDESMAID DRESS

Many brides decide they want control over choosing the bridesmaids' dresses. A bride will be aiming to pick out dresses that accent her wedding décor rather than going by the individual bridesmaids' preferences, sizes, and styles as her primary guide.

It will benefit you both if you politely offer to help her choose the bridesmaids' dresses. Just be sure to be extremely tactful because the bridesmaids' dresses have been a source of wedding jokes for many years.

Look at your suggestions regarding the bridesmaids' dresses as the voice of reason in the midst of increasing stress. Bear in mind everything you know about the other bridesmaids, especially their range in terms of size and what you know about their style.

Suggest that the bride pick out a number of different styles and then offer to go over her choices with her. There are two major factors to consider: age and dress size.

There may be a large discrepancy in the ages of the bridesmaids. If this is the case, try to choose a dress that is appropriate for all ages within the group. Remember that a cutting-edge style that looks fabulous on an eighteen-year-old bridesmaid may not look as good on a more mature bridesmaid.

A large age gap translates into less fashion experimentation. The greater the age range, the more classic the dress style should be.

You may also be aware of a great difference in dress sizes among the bridesmaids. If this is the case, be sure to make it a primary point when discussing dresses with the bride. A spaghetti strap dress with a fitted bodice may look great on a size six but may cause the woman who is a size sixteen to be traumatized by the wedding experience.

Since the bride really wants everyone to remember her wedding fondly, suggest that she choose a style that will look good and that will be comfortable for all the bridesmaids in her wedding party.

Another alternative is to suggest slightly different styles for each bridesmaid. The bride can adjust the color and style of each dress to flatter each bridesmaid. Ultimately, the bridesmaids should all look elegant, stylish, and classy. Of course, the style should be dictated by the overall style of the wedding. To get the ball rolling, pick up a stack of bridal magazines and tear out a bunch of different style bridesmaid dresses that appeal to you and that you think will work for some or all of the bridesmaids.

You should keep a number of factors in mind when looking through dress styles, including the general tone of the wedding and the season. Don't pick off the shoulder, backless dresses for the dead of winter or heavy velvet for an outdoor summer wedding.

Try to collect as many specifics as possible from the bride. What style shoes would she prefer? Does she want to dye the shoes to match the color of the gown, or would she prefer each bridesmaid simply choose a basic shoe style? (Remember, if dying the shoes, buy one size larger as the process can cause the shoes to shrink.)

What does she expect in terms of makeup? Is the bride happy for the bridesmaids to do their own makeup, or does she have a makeup artist who will be on hand the day of the wedding?

Keep in mind that the bridesmaids are responsible for paying for their dresses, alterations, shoes, handbags, nails, makeup, and accessories.

A bridesmaid's dress can cost anywhere from $150 to $500; shoes from $50 to $300; and makeup and accessories from $50 to $200. Add this on to the expense of traveling and hotel for any out-of-town bridesmaids, and you are talking about a major expense.

Once you have the general cost of the dress, makeup, and shoes and any information about jewelry, e-mail all the bridesmaids and ask them to respond either with an order, including a check, or any specific problems they may have paying for their dress.

Find out exactly when the dresses must be ordered and ensure all the girls have completed this in a suitable amount of time.

Once the dresses are ordered, plan dates for the first fitting, the second fitting, the final fitting, shoe shopping, and picking up the dresses.

Make sure there is enough time scheduled for that second and third fitting in case it turns out that someone's dress fits less than perfectly.

This means every bridesmaid should pick up her dress well in advance of the wedding date. Just give out the deadline for having the final alterations made and the dress completed.

Helping the bride choose her bridesmaids' dresses is one of the luckiest tasks a maid of honor has. Take full advantage of it to assure that you and all the other bridesmaids look radiant!

"*Happiness is what happens to us when we try to make someone else happy.*"

- Anonymous

Chapter Four

WEDDING DAY MAKEUP, HAIR, AND NAILS

As maid of honor you are responsible for getting your own makeup, hair, and nails done, making sure that the other bridesmaids have their hair and makeup done, and helping the bride with her hair and makeup. This is all a part of your job description. Phew! What a lot of (waterproof) mascara!

Ask the bride if she wants to find a professional makeup artist or if she wants to do her own makeup. It is a good idea to go to several large department stores and get a few free consultations for both of you. Be aware that it is customary for bridesmaids to pay for their own hair, makeup, and nails—so look for a line of cosmetics that are affordable for yourself, the other bridesmaids, and the bride.

Think of skincare, makeup, nails, and hairstyle as one complete package that must be attended to at the right point on the wedding timeline. Everyone in the wedding party naturally wants to look gorgeous on the big day, especially the bride. But stress can take a toll on skin (think breakouts), on hair (think straw-like texture), and on nails (think splitting, breaking, and peeling...or the possibility you have bitten them).

There are simple things you, the bridesmaids, and the bride can do in order to look radiant for the big day.

Skincare

For starters, if you or any of the wedding party, especially the bride, has any kind of a chronic skin problem, deal with it as soon as possible by seeing a dermatologist. There are effective medications and quick fixes available.

If you think her skin is less than perfect and if the bride asks for your advice, consider finding a recommended spa in your area and booking a series of custom facials at least once a month, anywhere from five to three months in advance of the wedding day.

A good facial should include the basics of cleansing, exfoliating, steaming, mask, and moisturizing. The spa should feel like a haven of serenity, and your facial should be an hour where you feel pampered and completely relaxed. If you feel tense, or worse, as if you are undergoing some medieval torture, find another salon!

Ask the therapist to work out a skin care regimen for you that is tailored to your skin type and stick to it! Sometimes facials can make your face break out afterwards because the extraction brings the oils the surface of the skin, so be sure to schedule your last facial no later than two weeks before the day of the wedding. (Remember to tell the therapist the specific date of the wedding.)

You can also prepare a do-it-yourself skin care routine to bring your skin to its radiant potential. Use a gentle cleanser that is not drying—you do not want to create patchy skin or parched lines! Find a good facial scrub with microbeads to exfoliate the skin; there are a number of at-home microdermabrasion kits on the market now that will leave you with polished, radiant skin.

Toners should be gentle and hydrating, and go easy on the moisturizer unless you have extremely dry skin. The aim is for your skin to look and feel soft, healthy, and radiant, not made-up.

Also an excellent idea is to fake it! Spray tans are a great way to look healthy and to even out your complexion. Remember to have a couple of trials done before the wedding day—nobody wants to see an orange streaky bride or bridesmaid on the day!

The best way to remove excess fake tan is lemon juice, salt, and water on an exfoliating cloth.

Wedding Day Hair

Rule number one: never change your hairstyle before the wedding. This applies particularly to the bride! It is nerve-wracking enough changing your hairstyle when you do not have to appear in front of an audience.

If you are truly unhappy with your style or color, plan to experiment a good six months in advance.

Find a hairdresser who makes you look fantastic with a cut that is natural and flattering to the shape of your face and your style, and then be loyal to him or her. Ask about the products you should use for your type of hair, and make sure you know how to style your hair at home.

Get your last trim and color done around one to two weeks before the wedding, and consider booking your hairdresser for the wedding day so he or she can make sure your style is perfect.

As maid of honor, check in with all the other bridesmaids and make sure they have arrangements to get their hair done for the wedding. As tactfully as possible, try to find out their plans.

If one bridesmaid has decided the time has come for her to dye her hair eggplant, do everything you can to change her mind, even if it means showing up at the hairdresser and throwing yourself on her mercy!

Also check in with the bride and ask if you can be of any assistance. Find out if she has a trusted hairdresser and if she knows how she wants her hair styled. If she wants to try several different styles, offer to go along with her to appointments. Be tactful when you offer your opinion, but be honest!

Your stylist's job is to help you find the right cut and style for your face, dress, and overall look. However, there are things that you should avoid such as big hair!

Big, teased, over-styled hair is only appropriate if the bride is having a fifties-theme wedding. Instead, go for a sleek, simple, polished look.

Another factor to consider is the staying power of your style. Aim for a style that will make it through the reception, including dancing barefoot into the wee hours! Putting your hair up with a few romantic tendrils floating around your face is a safe yet glamorous choice. You can also choose a style that is half up and half down. This look is romantic, but it also appears very youthful, so keep in mind the look you are trying to achieve. If the wedding is being held outdoors, you may want to avoid a style where your hair is all down.

If a strong wind comes up, you could end up with a knotted, tangled mess!

If you have decided on a style where your hair is up, wash your hair the night before. It makes it easier to work with the next day, and most stylists prefer to work with hair that has some natural oils in it.

Decide if you are going to do your hair by yourself on the wedding day, go to a salon, or have the stylist come to you. Just be sure to try out stylists at least three months in advance so you have plenty of time to find someone who gives you the look that is perfect for your face and dress.

If you choose to go to a salon, bear in mind the advantage of having everything done there at the same time—your hair, makeup, and nails.

And if you have found the perfect salon, spread the word to the other bridesmaids. Check in the night before and the morning of the wedding day to make sure everything is going smoothly.

Be prepared with a backup plan if someone's stylist has suddenly run off with his colorist! Have the name of your own stylist and one or two other stylists who are willing to go to their clients in case of any last minute emergencies.

Remember also to wear a top that has buttons or a zip down the front. The last thing you want to do is pull all your beautiful hair down and wipe off your makeup whilst taking off a roll-neck sweater!

THE WEDDING MANICURE

The day before the wedding, get a spa manicure. This usually includes a paraffin treatment, buffing, filing, exfoliating, and, of course, polishing. The bridesmaids' nails should complement the bride's nails but not overpower hers. Forget the lightning bolts and five-inch-long talons! Go for a French manicure or ask for a subtle color such as sheer pink or a pearlized off-white.

WEDDING DAY MAKEUP

Weddings are occasions that are documented by photographs, lots and lots of photographs! Whether the wedding is held indoors or outdoors, you want the light to reveal your natural beauty and radiant, clear skin. This requires careful makeup application.

Besides finding a makeup artist for yourself several weeks before the wedding, as maid of honor, go along with the bride as she tries out different makeup product lines and artists. Consider yourself as head of quality control and keep a watchful eye over what the makeup artist is doing. Encourage the bride to stay as natural and as close to her current look as possible and follow the same rule for yourself.

It is a good idea to go with the bride as you both try different products and looks. This way you can offer feedback and get hers at the same time.

Once the bride finds a look she likes, take notes about the application of the makeup and ask the makeup artist for a color chart; these are usually drawings of the face that indicate what color goes where.

Many makeup artists in salons and department stores can be booked for the day of the wedding, so if you and the bride find someone you think is brilliant, consider booking him or her. Looking fantastic on this day is a great investment.

During the process of finding the right makeup colors and style, you and the bride may decide on certain colors to match the bridesmaids' dresses. If this is the case, it is your responsibility to spread the word and make sure all the bridesmaids know what kind and color makeup they need to get and where to get it. Remember, every bridesmaid is financially responsible for her dress, shoes, accessories, hair, nails, and makeup. The only exception is if the bride offers on her own to help out.

Once you have your makeup and the bride's makeup done to both your satisfaction, look at the results in different lights. Go outside with a mirror and examine your makeup in the same light that will be present during the ceremony and during the reception.

Never be offended if the bride hates the makeup you suggested once she gets out into the bright sunlight of the rose garden where her ceremony will be held. Just get out your cotton balls and makeup remover and begin the process again.

If you are doing the bride's makeup and your own, practice, practice, practice! Then do the exact same thing on the day of the wedding, and you can feel confident that both you and the bride will be beautiful in any light.

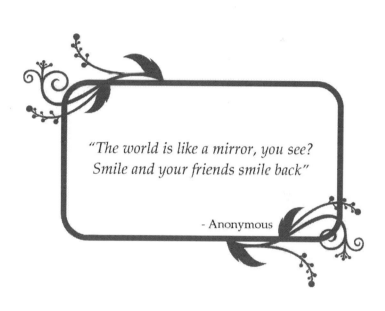

"The world is like a mirror, you see?
Smile and your friends smile back"

- Anonymous

Chapter Five

PLANNING A BRIDAL SHOWER

The bridal shower, traditionally hosted by the maid of honor, is a once-in-a-lifetime event, so it must be absolutely perfect! It must be spectacular and dazzling and filled with joy, hugs, and "showers" of delightful gifts like leopard print sheets and those little seashell soaps.

Sometimes, a bride will have numerous showers hosted by different groups of people, so you must sit down with her, find out what her plans are, and get a guest list for the shower you are hosting. If she is attending other bridal showers, try to get an idea of what they might be like.

For example, do they have any special themes, are they formal or informal, and so forth.

As the maid of honor, use your deep and personal knowledge of the bride to design a shower for her that she will never forget. This is the event in the whole wedding extravaganza where you can truly express you feelings and your understanding of her as a person and as your friend.

So, if she has always wanted to go on a midnight sail, or swim with the dolphins, or skip amongst the wooly mammoths at the Museum of National History, this bridal shower is the perfect opportunity to make her dreams come true!

Of course, she may be the kind of bride who goes for a laid-back, country western barbecue bash or has always admired your very own Japanese rock garden you have labored over for the last two decades.

You will find, as you begin to explore venues, that there are seemingly infinite resources for hosting a bridal shower.

All you need to get going with this oh-so-important obligation is good judgment, a dash of intuition, a realistic budget, and an appropriate guest list.

The Guest List

Compile a tentative guest list before you sit down with the bride. A large part of the whole wedding event is about the people who are attending, and the bridal shower is no exception. You must invite certain guests to the bride's shower, such as her mother, future mother-in-law, grandmother, aunts, future sisters-in-law and possibly her coworkers (unless there is a separate shower being held by her office buddies).

Even if the bride has had a food fight with her mother-in-law over the caterer and her mother-in-law prevailed, decorum dictates a bride's mother-in-law is invited to the shower. (But go ahead and have it catered by the caterer who lost the first round. The bride will love you for it!) Immediate female family members of both the bride and groom's families should be invited as well as close friends of the bride and the wedding party.

Anyone invited to the bridal shower customarily should be invited to the wedding, but everyone invited to the wedding does not have to be invited to the shower.

The idea is to make as many people as happy as you can without going crazy or bankrupt and to step on as few toes as possible.

Of course, the objective is to shower the guest of honor with gifts, so the bride's happiness must never be forgotten! Just warn her in advance to steer clear of relative so-and-so, or keep your own eyes peeled and be ready to offer a gently guiding arm if two feuding females appear to be about to lock horns. Be prepared with a big smile and copious quantities of shower punch and champagne.

THE BUDGET

This is NOT the fun part. You must come up with a realistic budget and then figure out where and how to get the finances together. Your budget is comprised of the cost for the shower site if you are renting, food and drink, entertainment, invitations, party favors, and gifts.

Your largest expense will be renting a party space, so if you plan to host the shower in any place other than your own home, you have some research to do first. Once you find a few places that you like, get the rental price, but make sure you know exactly what is included in their fee.

Food and drink will be your next largest expense. For invitations, go to a printer and check out their preprinted shower invitations. Get a few different cards and quotes. Then call a meeting of the other bridesmaids and ask if any would be willing to contribute to this event.

Remember, however, that it is your obligation as maid of honor to host and finance the bridal shower.

You might decide you want to all chip in on a large gift if you know for sure that there is something both the bride and the groom would love.

One last word of advice when gathering with the other bridesmaids to discuss the shower: remember that you, the maid of honor, are in charge. This means that if the discussion becomes anything less than cheery, you have the final say!

Shower Venues

Traditionally, the bridal shower is held in the maid of honor's home. But many weddings have veered away from tradition, and the shower should be no exception, particularly if you live in a fifth floor walk-up studio apartment!

There are many unusual and trustworthy places to host a shower. On the trustworthy side, consider a favorite restaurant with a roaring fireplace, a local bar with a dance floor and pool tables, or even an elegant tea house. For unusual ideas, think castles, conservatories, yachts, country clubs, even bowling alleys.

Enlist another bridesmaid or two to go around and check out venues. Some places will include a complete menu and open bar while others expect you to cater the event yourself. Also, find out how long you are allowed to rent the space for.

Always be led by the personality and style of the bride. Remember that a bridal shower is a celebration of love found and the devotion of friendship. Keep this one goal in mind, and you will be sure to throw a shower that your good friend and bride will always remember as one of the pivotal moments of her life.

BRIDAL SHOWER THEMES AND GAMES

Depending on the personality and style of the bride, you may want to organize the shower around a theme. There are numerous themes to choose from. Some themes revolve around a type of gift, such as a:

- ✺ Honeymoon Shower
- ✺ Linen Shower
- ✺ Lingerie Shower
- ✺ Bed and Bath Shower
- ✺ Pamper the Bride Shower
- ✺ Stock the Bar Shower
- ✺ Stock the Kitchen Shower
- ✺ Garden Supplies Shower
- ✺ Gift Basket Shower
- ✺ Tea or Coffee Cup Shower
- ✺ Money Tree Shower

Other themes can dictate the type of food, decorations, and entertainment you choose, such as a:

- Western Barbecue Shower
- Fifties Soda Shop Shower
- Backyard Pool Party Shower
- Elegant Tea Party Shower
- International Style Shower
- Garden Party Shower
- Hearts Shower

Choosing a theme can make the planning and gift giving much easier. Just make sure to pick one that will complement the bride's unique taste and style.

At some showers, shower games are played.

This works best if there are guests who do not know each other well. A few lighthearted games can help break the ice and give guests a chance to meet.

Have the bride fill out an information sheet about herself, such as what is her favorite food, color, vacation place, sport, place she wants to live, designer, painter, style of house, and so forth. Phrase the information as questions: If you could live anywhere in the world, where would it be? What is your favorite place to eat lunch? If you could buy a single painting, which one would it be?

Then give the same questions to each guest and have them fill in what they believe the bride's answers will be. When everyone has filled out their forms, go around the room and have each guest read her answers. Have the bride go last. Give out a prize for the guest who comes closest to the bride's answers, and have another prize for the answers the bride likes the best.

You can find literally hundreds of shower games at bridal shower sites online. If you decide to play some of these games, aim to get them in before eating and choose only three or four that you think your particular guests will truly enjoy.

If you are planning on playing some shower games, make sure to have a bunch of extra party favors on hand for game prizes.

INVITATIONS

Sending out invitations that reflect the theme or style of the shower sets the tone and makes it easier for everyone to remember the date. Printers have large catalogs of preprinted shower invitations that include the RSVP card and return envelopes. All you have to do is add the date, time, location, and any information about gifts to the preprinted notes.

If you are especially close to the bride, consider handmade cards as they add a unique, personal touch. You can make simple yet elegant invitations from a large choice of beautiful card and paper stocks. Or choose some striking stationary that reflects something about the bride, such as her passion for Hello Kitty or starfish.

Send out invitations a month in advance so those long-distance guests will have the time to make plans. Request the return of RSVPs no later than two weeks before the shower date.

FOOD AND BEVERAGES

If you are hosting the shower in an outside party space, find out if the place has a caterer. If so, they will usually offer you a variety of menus.

If you are making the food yourself, you can design the menu around the time of day or the shower theme. For example, serve tea sandwiches and an assortment of exotic teas for a tea party shower; serve burgers and french fries for a fifties soda shop shower.

For an afternoon shower, go with platters of cold cuts, tuna, chicken and seafood salads, pasta salads, and green salads. For an elegant, sit-down dinner shower, prepare at least one meat, one seafood, and two vegetable dishes.

Catering is always a good option if you are feeling stressed or are not too sure of your culinary skills. If you do plan to cook, you can prepare some foods in advance the day before the shower.

Beverages should never be mixed until the first guests arrive.

Consider asking a few bridesmaids if they would contribute a dish, and do not forget the shower cake. There are numerous recipes and suggestions for decorating shower cakes available online. Or go to your favorite bakery and design a personalized masterpiece with your local baker.

Shower Favors

It is customary for the hostess to give out party favors to her guests at the shower. These gifts are usually given either as guests arrive or when they leave. If you plan on playing any shower games, party favors can be used as prizes for winning. Design your party favors around your theme or with the bride's taste in mind. For example, if you are throwing a garden party shower, consider giving small, potted plants tied with ribbons or in hand-painted pots as favors.

For a pamper the bride shower, you could give beautiful soaps and luxurious lotions as favors; for a pool party, consider wild sunglasses or delectable body oils. Consider mood rings and charm bracelets for a fifties soda shop shower and dozens of different teacups for a tea party shower. There are tons of novelty and party shops where you can buy all of your shower supplies in one place.

This may not only make your life easier and less stressful, but it will ensure that everything is coordinated.

The bridal shower is about the bride. It should be a relaxed and joyful experience where the bride's friends and family celebrate her happiness and wish her the best for her future life. This means the maid of honor must have enough energy to participate and have fun!

Keep this in the forefront of your thinking when planning the bridal shower and never hesitate to let someone else do the work, such as catering the food, if it means it will free you up to celebrate with abandon!

"We come to love not by finding a perfect person, but by learning to see an imperfect person perfectly."

- Anonymous

Chapter Six

PLANNING A BACHELORETTE PARTY

A newer tradition than the bridal shower is a bachelorette party for the bride. This party is similar to the groom's "stag party" in which the bride and her bridesmaids celebrate her last days of being single by getting wild and crazy. Put together by the maid of honor, this party may not be as traditional as the bridal shower, but in some ways it is more essential.

It gives the bride and her best friends a night out to blow off steam, stress, and worries and most importantly, to celebrate the end of an era in the bride's life.

The bachelorette party is typically a bit on the wild side and is the perfect occasion for some serious girl-bonding.

As maid of honor, it is your obligation to plan this unusual event, and you will find a wide assortment of ideas, games, entertainment ideas, and novelty gift ideas in magazines, books, and Web sites.

Before you dive headfirst into the mountain of condom veils, exotic male dancers, and erotic party cakes, it is a good idea to figure out what style of party you plan to throw. Decide first whether you want to plan a classy, elegant affair, or a down-and-dirty, on-the-trashy-side bash. Once you figure out the general tone, you can then decide on appropriate venues, decorations, entertainment, and gifts.

The most crucial factor in throwing a successful bachelorette party is making sure that everyone invited will be comfortable with your plans. Call together a brainstorming session with all the bridesmaids and have several different places and entertainment options ready to present.

Knock around your ideas, juggling the details, until you find a plan that everyone is enthusiastic about. In this party, manners and etiquette are not the focus; having a blast is the ultimate goal.

Consult with the bride about the guest list. Typically, all the bridesmaids are invited, but the bride may want to invite other guests as well. Once you know who to invite, contact everyone well in advance; it will not be easy to find an evening that is available for everyone on the guest list.

Once you have the date and the general tone, decide on how you will finance your party. It is customary for all the bridesmaids to chip in for this event with the maid of honor coordinating and directing all the details. Figure out how much everything will cost and then split those costs evenly. You may want to include a group gift along with a party space, invitations, transportation, food and beverages, decorations, and novelty items.

If you decide to host the party in your own house, plan to foot the main part of the bill and then consider asking the bridesmaids to contribute food and drink.

Since this party is not as formal as the bridal shower, printed invitations are not required. You can simply e-mail or telephone everyone with the date and details. However, a printed, funny bachelorette party invitation can set the tone and give everyone an idea of what to expect.

One of the purposes of this party is to put the bride in the spotlight. For example, guests often plan to buy the bride a goofy bridal veil or novelty crown and insist she wear it all night in public.

Just make sure that your teasing is meant affectionately and that the bride thinks it is as funny as you do!

Popular venues for hosting your party include bars, nightclubs, strip clubs, weekend vacation spots, gambling casinos, spas, cruises, hotels, exclusive restaurants, and private homes. If you plan to barhop, either assign a designated driver, rent a limo, go by cab, or travel first to an area where there are a lot of different bars within walking distance.

There are a number of ways to keep costs down. If you are hosting the party at a private home, keep the food and decorations simple and have everyone contribute a food dish and a bottle of wine, champagne, or liquor. If you are going out on the town, have everyone meet at a private home to share drinks and gossip first. Split the responsibility for bringing hors d'oeuvres, food, and liquor amongst the bridesmaids instead of buying food or having the party catered.

While it is a good idea for guests to give the bride some serious gifts, a bachelorette party demands a bunch of humorous, wacky presents.

Get together with the other bridesmaids and pool your combined knowledge of the bride to come up with the perfect gag gift to commemorate the occasion.

A customary "serious" gift that can never fail to please is beautiful lingerie. Other ideas include:

- ❧ Tickets for the bride and groom to a play, concert, ballet, or show of any kind depending on the bride and groom's taste

- ❧ Gift certificates to a favorite store

- ❧ Gift certificate to a day of beauty and relaxation at a spa

- ❧ A romantic weekend away at a resort or a bed and breakfast

- ❧ Satin sheet sets

Another important element of the bachelorette party is to remember the bride's past and to fantasize about her future. There are numerous ways you can commemorate her memories.

One great way is to have all the bridesmaids assemble some of their personal pictures of the bride and make a tongue-in-cheek captioned scrapbook for her. Another idea is to buy a beautiful blank journal and, together, write her a "this is your life" book. If you are planning a party at a private home, create a special mixed drink and name it for the bride.

Whatever style of party and venue you choose to go with, the goal should be to make the bride feels special and treasured.

Another integral part of a bachelorette party is playing games. You will find innumerable suggestions and game kits in party stores or on Web sites. Remember, whatever you choose, make sure the bride and guests are comfortable participating.

This party should be a sizzling night the bride and her friends will never forget, so whatever your responsibilities are, the most important one is to have a fabulous time!

*"Love one another and you will be happy.
It's as simple and difficult as that."*

- Michael Leunig

Chapter Seven

ON THE BIG DAY

Finally, the day of the wedding arrives! This is the time to take a lot of calming, deep breaths and get serious.

The bride will be depending on her maid of honor for some very important tasks, but most of all, she will look to you for support and reassurance.

Even if you are on the verge of self-combustion with nervous energy, it is very important that you remain calm and be a pillar of emotional support for your best friend.

Try to anticipate what the bride will need most. If you know that she reaches for certain things when she is stressed, such as ice cream, make sure to have a few pints on hand.

Make a list in advance of everything that you will need to check on the day of the wedding, such as the flower delivery and perhaps the entertainment, and then start delegating! Pick a few trusted bridesmaids and divvy up the responsibilities so that you are free to give your undivided attention to the bride.

Speaking of bridesmaids, you will now have switch into high gear, get out your megaphone, and make sure they are all pulled together and ready to go.

Call up the bridesmaids first thing in the morning and check that everyone's dress is ready and still fits, make sure each bridesmaid has the right bouquet, remind everyone exactly what they have to do and when they have to do it, and generally be prepared to rally the troops.

The maid of honor should arrive at the bride's house first to help her get ready. It is a good idea to plan a breakfast as the bride will undoubtedly be too nervous, or completely forget, to eat.

Since one of your main jobs is to keep the bride calm, getting her to eat will go a long way toward making sure she doesn't keel over in the course of the day.

However, plan to sit down with her (and other bridesmaids and helpers) to eat before she puts on any bridal gear.

You definitely want to avoid the possibility of the bride dropping a jam-topped scone in her lap when she is dressed! This goes for you and any other bridesmaids present, too.

Be prepared to assist the bride in whatever way she requires. This may include running last minute errands, answering the phone, arranging transportation for the bridesmaids, providing encouragement and repeatedly telling the bride how fabulous she looks, and checking on guests and other details of the wedding—all without bothering the bride with anything.

Plan to get ready while the bride is busy, but always be within shouting distance. If the bride is having her hair styled and her makeup done professionally, this is a good time to take care of business unless you are also having your hair and makeup done at the same time.

A good tip to remember is to make sure to cover the bride's face, and your own, with a cloth or even a pillowcase before she puts on her gown. The last thing she needs is her blusher smeared on her ivory lace!

One of your responsibilities is to help the bride get dressed. This means helping her into her dress and veil and then arranging them so you can both see what they should look like as she prepares to walk down the aisle. Spread out the train a few feet and have her practice walking in her gown.

You may have to touch up her makeup and fix her hair throughout the day (and the evening), so pack the essentials you will need before you leave for the ceremony.

Also be sure to take along for emergencies:

- A small sewing kit
- Pain killers
- Money
- Tweezers
- Pins and safety pins
- Hairspray
- Buttons
- Cotton wool
- Band Aids
- Snacks
- Bottled water
- Camera
- Mirror
- Perfume
- Moisturizer
- Dental floss
- Nail polish
- Nail file and clippers
- Stockings
- Emergency phone numbers
- Sticky tape
- Chalk or baby powder
- Matches

- Straws
- Sanitary wear
- Handkerchief
- Glue
- A wrap of some kind in case the temperature drops
- Your own makeup essentials
- Breath mints
- Hand wipes
- Hair brush and comb
- Extra hair pins
- Spot remover
- Sunscreen for an outside wedding
- A small tube of hand cream
- Tissues
- Umbrella

And include anything else that you can think of to help you both sail through the day, shining and looking refreshed. Before the limo arrives to take you to the ceremony, call ahead and deal with any last-minute disasters and be sure the bride hears nothing about them! Keep assuring her that everything is running exactly as planned and that she is absolutely stunning.

Be prepared to keep repeating this even if the bride's face has turned chalk white. Help her to concentrate on the meaning of the day by doing everything you can to screen out all distractions.

If it works out that the bride is getting dressed at another location or that someone else (such as her mother) is helping her, make sure that you arrive at the ceremony at least thirty minutes before she does. Be on top of coordinating when the other bridesmaids will arrive and try to get everyone assembled before the bride shows up. Having to wait for members of the wedding party to arrive is one stress that should (and can) be avoided.

You must also make sure everyone shows up where they need to be for pre-wedding photographs. Check in with the photographer a few days before the wedding date and get the exact details. Then keep on top of everyone who is on-call and be there early to shepherd your crew before the waterfall, rose trellis, or photo backdrop.

One last thing before we dive into the specifics for the ceremony and the reception: make sure that the bride gives you the groom's wedding ring before you leave for the ceremony. You will be responsible for handing it over at the appropriate moment during the marriage ceremony.

"Do not wish to be anything but what you are, and try to be that perfectly."

- St Frances De Sales

Chapter Eight

THE CEREMONY AND THE RECEPTION

As soon as you get to the ceremony site, things will shift into high gear. The more prepared you feel, the calmer you will be. The ceremony is the most nerve-wracking event for the bride and groom, so be prepared for major jitters. Remind the bride that there is a great party following the ceremony and plan to offer her tons of emotional support before she walks down the aisle.

Consider going over in advance everything you must attend to in terms of the ceremony and the reception. It is a good idea to make a quick checklist that you can refer to when things start heating up. Find out if the first set of photographs is being taken before or after the ceremony and plan to arrive with plenty of time to speak with the other bridesmaids and help everyone get to the photo shoot on time.

You might gather all the bridesmaids together and go over, one last time, what everyone is supposed to do. You will be responsible for holding a number of things during the ceremony, such as the bridal bouquet during the vows and the groom's ring.

You will be holding onto the real ring; the ring bearer traditionally carries a fake representation. Put the groom's ring on your thumb to be sure you don't misplace it.

One of your first obligations will probably be signing the marriage license along with the best man. Make sure you know where he is and stay with the bride so you are around when the license is ready.

THE CEREMONY

The time has come to take your place in the processional down the aisle. Help the bride first by arranging her veil, bustle, and train. Make sure she is comfortable and can walk steadily before you take your place.

Take a few deep breaths before following the bridesmaids down the aisle. Since you are not in the actual hot seat, remind yourself that you are doing this to have fun. Consciously relax, breathe deeply, and smile! Hold your bouquet at your waist with your elbows bent but relaxed and walk slowly. The bride can get away with looking panic stricken; her maid of honor should be radiating joy and good wishes for her close friend.

Keep a natural expression on your face and don't pay attention to the congregation. Above all, try not to respond in any way to people coughing, sneezing, sobbing, or children crying.

When the bride reaches the altar, discreetly arrange her dress and train so that it looks good. Keep your attention focused on the bride and groom and don't crane your neck to see the congregation. Take the bride's bouquet for the ceremony and pass her the groom's ring at the appropriate point.

After the ceremony and the kiss, take your part in the recessional back down the aisle. The order is usually the bride and groom, the flower girl and ring bearer, the maid of honor and the best man, followed by the other bridesmaids arm-in-arm with the ushers. If the ceremony is Jewish, the recessional order is a little different: bride and groom, bride's parents, groom's parents, attendants who are children, maid of honor, and, finally, the other bridesmaids and the ushers.

The final responsibility of the maid of honor at the ceremony is to take your place in the receiving line.

This tradition is arranged so that the bride and groom and their wedding party can greet each guest personally. At large weddings, the receiving line is sometimes held at the reception site.

Ask the bride in advance where she would like you to stand in the receiving line. Sometimes the bride asks her bridesmaids to circulate among the guests and make sure everyone knows where to go after the ceremony or, if the receiving line is held at the reception site, to make sure the guests all know where their tables are.

If asked to stand in the receiving line, you will usually stand next to the bride on her left. Greet everyone warmly but briefly.

Phew! It is now time to party!

THE RECEPTION

When you get to the reception site, find the bride and consider taking her aside so she can calm down. Bring a glass of champagne with you and a lot of tissues! Tell her how beautiful the ceremony was and expect her to be very emotional. If the bride decides to change dresses, help her out of her gown and into her new attire.

Find out in advance where you can store the wedding dress and then pack it away so that it does not get soiled. Help the bride fix her hair and makeup again. This is a good time to share a small drink and deep breaths together before you make an appearance at the reception.

With the other bridesmaids, help the guests find their tables. You will probably be seated at the bride's table with the rest of the wedding party, sitting to the left of the groom.

If you have brought along a date, find out in advance if he can sit with you; most likely, there won't be room at the bride's table, and he will be seated nearby.

At more formal weddings, there is often a kind of processional into the reception area where a toastmaster introduces each member of the wedding party and then presents the bride and groom as a married couple.

Once you hear your name called, it is time to make your entrance, smiling and perhaps waving at people you know. In this processional, walk quickly, keep smiling, and take your seat at the bride's table as soon as you can without falling off your heels.

You will most likely be expected to make a toast at the reception after the best man makes his toast. Plan this toast carefully in advance and practice it until you are comfortable and can speak from the heart.

If it makes you feel secure, bring along a few notes that you can glance down at, but make sure that you maintain eye contact with various people when you are speaking.

This toast should be different from the one you made at the rehearsal dinner. You are now speaking about the bride after she has gotten married. Refer to your long friendship and your closeness, remark about how honored you are to make a toast at her wedding, speak a little about the groom and how great he is for the bride, add a dash of funny, personal anecdotes, and wind up wishing them a long and happy future.

Try to keep your voice steady and your posture straight. In the same manner as the rehearsal dinner toast, when it is your turn, stand and raise your glass. Do not clink silverware on the wineglasses to get everyone's attention. Just stand quietly without twirling your hair or shuffling your feet and wait for the guests to quiet down.

Make your speech as personal and specific as possible without embarrassing yourself or making the bride uncomfortable. The most important factor is that you speak confidently, so tailor your toast to what feels natural.

Whatever happens during your toast, let it go afterwards. No one will feel good if you gripe about how you forgot the groom's name. Remember that the point of your toast is to celebrate the bride and her new marriage, not to draw attention to yourself.

Try to find out beforehand when the dancing will begin. Sometimes it starts after the first course, and sometimes it does not begin until the entire meal is finished. Customarily, the bride and groom have the first dance to their special song, joined next by their parents. The bridesmaids follow, dancing with the ushers, while you dance the first time with the best man.

If you are uncomfortable dancing with many pairs of eyes on you, you might try to arrange a few mini-rehearsals with the best man. This is probably a good idea if he is a stranger to you or if you are expected to dance formally and skillfully.

Many times the bride and groom actually take dance lessons to ensure that their first appearance goes off smoothly. The more information you get in advance, the more graceful and relaxed you will appear.

During the reception, mingle among the guests and try to make sure everyone has what they need. Check in frequently with the bride; offer her reassurances and your shoulder and ears and try to keep her adrenaline flowing a bit more steadily.

The cake-cutting tradition usually signals that the reception is drawing to a close. It will sometimes be followed by the bouquet toss. Again, talk to the bride about this in advance.

Today, this tradition is sometimes considered outdated and is eliminated. If the bride and her bridesmaids decide to keep it just for the fun factor, you must participate! Be prepared; never turn and flee if you see the bouquet coming at you! Just catch it and keep smiling, no matter what your circumstances are. Keep remembering that the point of this tradition, as with all the other ones, is to have fun!

When you get the signal from the bride that she is preparing to leave with her new husband, assemble the other bridesmaids. You may be expected to help her gather her things together, especially if she is leaving directly for her honeymoon.

It is traditional to shower the bride and groom with good luck tokens, such as rice or rose petals, when they exit their reception. If this is planned, make sure to pass out handfuls to all the other bridesmaids and guests.

There may be an after-reception party planned. If so, make sure you know where it is and that all the other bridesmaids have this information if they plan to attend.

You have put in a lot of hard work, and you deserve to have a good time. Check in with the bride frequently and try to help her relax and have fun, too. Remember that this a joyous occasion, despite your many obligations, so don't forget to thoroughly enjoy yourself!

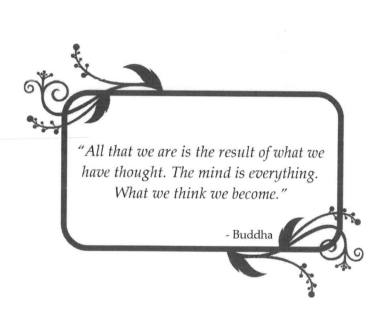

"All that we are is the result of what we have thought. The mind is everything. What we think we become."

- Buddha

Chapter Nine

SAMPLE TOASTS

Sample 1

When _____ first asked me to be her maid of honor, I was truly thrilled and honored. (You may consider adding a clause or two here about the nature of your relationship with the bride.) I still am honored. Though, I have to admit, after the initial thrill wore off, the realization hit me that at some point I would have to get up and give a speech, which was definitely less thrilling. I really racked my brain as to what to say.

Be funny, I thought. Well, that's easier said than done. Heck, _____ proves that every day. Believe it or not, (s)he actually thinks (s)he's funny! (You could mention the bride, the groom, or even a relative or the bride or groom here, if it is appropriate.)

Then I thought, just give them really good advice. Now that was something I could do:

Remember, always wear clean underwear.

If you have none left...well, why don't you do some laundry once in awhile!

Remember, look both ways before crossing the street.

Of course, just which two ways they are referring to, I am not sure, but it still sounds good.

Remember, don't ever give me a drink before giving a toast, ever again!

So perhaps, the advice thing didn't work out so well after all.

That's OK; I have other ideas.

I was told, "Say some nice things about the bride and groom."

Hmmm.

Ummm…

Hmmm…

Ummm…

Well, OK, let me get back to you on that one.

I guess by now _____ is rethinking her selection in a maid of honor, but luckily for me, it is really too late for her to do anything about it.

Oh, there you go, I just thought of something nice to say about _____… She was smart enough to pick me as her maid of honor. (You may consider adding a quick story here if there is an appropriate one about your adventures together.) But, getting back to the toast, I thought perhaps the best thing to do would be to find some amazing quote, some beautiful sentiment, and blow everyone away with it.

I spent quite a bit of time finding one and truly found the perfect one.

But then, after watching the ceremony, I realized the most beautiful sentiment of all was seeing _____ and _____ looking into each other's eyes.

I watched as two wonderful people pledged their love and their lives to each other, in front of their family and friends…and that blew me away.

I think we all were fortunate today as we were witness to a truly special moment. I ask that everyone please stand and raise your glasses. _____ and _____.

Thank you for allowing me to be a part of this very special day.

Thank you for allowing all of us to share in your love. May God bless you both, may your love for each other continue to grow, and may today be the first day of the rest of your lives, which should be filled with health, happiness, and love. _____ and _____, here's to you!

I would like to start out by acknowledging a very special lesson my grandmother taught me—a rule to live by, above all other rules. She said to me, "If you have nothing nice to say, say nothing." (Start to walk away as if you are done.) OK, just kidding. My grandmother actually used to say, "If you have nothing nice to say, sit next to me." Strange how everyone wanted to sit next to her.

Speaking of strange. Who picked out these bridesmaid dresses? I mean, clearly today is about _____. And she didn't want any of us to get a smidgen of the spotlight, and I must say, in these dresses, she accomplished just that!

It's almost like that TV show *What Not to Wear*, or *Bridesmaids Gone Wild*.

Come on now, _____, I am only kidding. They aren't really awful.

OK, OK, they really are, but that's not what we are here for tonight.

Tonight we are all here to celebrate the marriage of _____ and _____, two people who were clearly destined to be together.

Destined to be together—doesn't that just sound good? It was DESTINY. They were DESTINED.

Doesn't it really just mean that no one else would want either of them, so they had no choice but to get married?

I mean really, when you boil it right down to the bare facts, I'm pretty sure that's the case here.

But whatever the reason these two got together and got married, whether it be...destiny... chance...fate...a bottle of wine and no better prospects...a blank check from _____'s father. Whatever the reason, it doesn't matter. (Be sensitive here; judge which of the above items you include based on the history of the bride, the groom, and/or their family members.)

What matters is we are all here tonight for one very special reason.

To give gifts! So please, eat quickly, don't rack up a big bar tab, drop off your gifts on your way out, and drive safely.

In case of a sudden drop in pressure, airbags will drop from the overhead in front of you. (During this portion do the hand motions that a flight attendant would do on a flight.)

If we need to evacuate for any reason, there are aisle safety lights, or just follow the screaming flight attendant.

Now that you have been given that advice, let me share with you the advice I was given on how to give this toast. I was told things like: "Hey, just picture everyone in their underwear." And I got to tell you something. Some of you people should really rethink your underwear selections. I mean a red lace thong, really, Mr. _____, in the future please wear underwear with MUCH more material. (You may either mention the groom's father, or the bride's father, or select someone else to look at and fill in the blank.)

I was told, "Don't say anything embarrassing to the bride or groom." Well, if that's the case, they shouldn't have opened the bar before handing me the microphone! Alcohol + me + microphone = a recipe for disaster! (You may consider adding a quick story here if there is an appropriate one.)

Another wise person said, "Remember: KISS." Heck, I thought that meant I'd get a chance to make out with the best man, then, much to my dismay, I was told KISS means "keep it short, stupid."

Hey, I got the stupid part down, and one out of three ain't bad!

I have to say, the best advice I got was still my grandma's. And if you ain't got anything nice to say, say nothing at all.

So keeping it short, proving I'm stupid. Let's all just raise our glasses and give a toast to _____ and _____.

May your lives be full of happiness.
May your fridge be full of beer.
May your days be touched with sweetness.
And may your love grow throughout the years!

_____ and _____,
here's to you!

Tonight it is my true honor to be able to toast such a wonderful couple. It is so rare in this day and age to see such love and to truly know that it is a love that will last for a lifetime.

In a world that oftentimes seems out of control, where people sometimes seem to forget about patience and kindness, it is refreshing to see pure love.

When I see a love like _____ and _____ share, it reminds me of how much beauty can come, no matter the surroundings. (You may consider adding a quick story here if there is an appropriate one.)

A day like today reminds me of a saying. I believe Confucius said: "I am reminded of the lotus flower that grows from the mud. I am reminded of the butterfly that transforms from a caterpillar. I am reminded that Botox is truly a gift from God."

Tonight we are celebrating much more than the coming together of two lives. We are also celebrating the coming together of two families. (You may consider adding a quick story about the families here if there is an appropriate one.)

There are certainly going to be many ups and downs in the road ahead of you. But remember, if not for the downs, you would never be able to appreciate the ups.

There will certainly be many laughs and many tears. But if not for the tears, the laughs would seem less special.

There will be many losses and many victories. Remember to mourn the losses but also to celebrate the victories.

Remember how you feel tonight as there will surely be days you wonder what you were thinking.

Most of all, remember that every single person in this room loves you both and wishes you nothing but happiness and love.

So please join me in raising your glasses to _____ and _____.

To the happy couple, who share a love that most could only envy, few could ever match, and none could ever surpass.

_____ and _____, here's to you.

Sample 4

It is customary to start a toast with welcoming the family and friends of the bride and groom to the reception.

But tonight, I wanted to part from tradition and instead toast the truth.

So, rather than thank you each for coming, on behalf of the bride and groom, I will just say, "Thank you for your gifts." For after all, isn't that the real reason we have all been invited here? To give a gift.

Oh sure, the happy couple will try to claim that they wanted us to help them celebrate their union. Oh please, who are they kidding?

Their celebration doesn't happen until they get to the hotel room, and I don't think we'll be getting an invite there…will we?

The morning after talk would be much more interesting.

Weddings like that would actually help make men want to go to them rather than spend the entire car ride to the wedding getting a list of dos and don'ts from us ladies.

Oh, now men, you know what I mean. You know you were given your warnings.

Let's see a show of hands from the men in the room. How many of you here got "warnings" from your wife, girlfriend, mother, whomever, before you arrived?

Come on, be honest.

Those of you with your hands raised, I congratulate you on being bold enough to admit it, being man enough to raise your hand with no fear of the ramifications later. Oh, and believe me…there WILL be ramifications.

To you liars with your hands still down…I congratulate you because, unlike the schmucks with their hands in the air, you may actually get a little loving tonight!

Now for those of you wondering if I plan to say anything about the bride and groom tonight—get over it! The best man already did that! If you give me an open bar and a microphone, hey, you are asking for trouble! I cannot be held responsible.

But I would seriously like to say that it is an honor being here this evening as _____ and _____ celebrate their love for each other.

(You may consider adding a quick story here if there is an appropriate one about their relationship.)

At the ceremony, as I watched these two beautiful people join their lives together, I was surprised how much it touched me, sitting and watching _____ say, "I do." And it wasn't even preceded by "HEY, anyone want another beer?"!

The bride and I go way back. I cannot imagine what my life would have been like if she were not in it.

We have been through so much; we know each other's hopes and dreams, our accomplishments and failures, and our proudest moments and darkest secrets.

By the way, for $29.95 you can download some video of _____ off the Internet from WWW – IM A BIG MESS DOT COM.

Seriously though, I would like to congratulate _____ and _____ on their wedding day. Today truly is the first day of the rest of your lives.

Tonight is a magical night for you both, one that you are sure to look back on for a long time…and wonder why you asked me, of all people, to give a toast.

Now friends, family, invited guests, party crashers, people wondering what the heck you are doing here, please rise to your feet and lift your glasses.

For those of you not wearing antiperspirant—you know who you are and so do we—please only lift your glasses shoulder height. Let's lift our glasses and wish _____ and _____ many years of happiness, health, and love.

May God bless you and watch over you, may the rest of your lives be as special as tonight, and may you remember this toast as it is unlikely I will ever be asked to give another one.

_____ and _____, here's to you!

QUOTES WORTH QUOTING

People need loving the most when they deserve it
the least.

—JOHN HARRIGAN

Patience with others is love, patience with self is
hope, patience with God is faith.

— ADEL BESTAVROS

One word frees us of all the weight and pain of
life: that word is love.

—SOPHOCLES

Now join your hands and with your hands your
heart.

—WILLIAM SHAKESPEARE

Love one another and you will be happy. It's as
simple and as difficult as that.

—MICHAEL LEUNIG

Love is the triumph of imagination over
intelligence.

—HENRY LOUIS MENCKEN

Love is stronger than justice.

—STING

Love is an emotion experienced by the many and enjoyed by the few.

—GEORGE JEAN NATHAN

Love does not consist in gazing at each other, but in looking outward together in the same direction.

—ANTOINE DE SAINT-EXUPERY

Love cures people, both the ones who give it and the ones who receive it.

—DR. KARL MENNINGER

Life is to be fortified by many friendships. To love and to be loved is the greatest happiness of existence.

—SYDNEY SMITH

Life is the flower for which love is the honey.

—VICTOR HUGO

In the arithmetic of love, one plus one equals everything and two minus one equals nothing.

—MIGNON MCLAUGHLIN

A friend is one who knows us, but loves us anyway.

—FR. JEROME CUMMINGS

Everybody can be great...because anybody can serve. You don't have to have a college degree to serve. You don't have to make your subject and verb agree to serve. You only need a heart full of grace. A soul generated by love.

—MARTIN LUTHER KING, JR.

He to whom this emotion is a stranger, who can no longer pause to wonder and stand rapt in awe, is as good as dead: his eyes are closed.

—ALBERT EINSTEIN

Hatred paralyzes life; love releases it. Hatred confuses life; love harmonizes it. Hatred darkens life; love illumines it.

—MARTIN LUTHER KING, JR.

I have found the paradox that if I love until it hurts, then there is no hurt, but only more love.

—MOTHER TERESA

The love we give away is the only love we keep.

—ELBERT HUBBARD

To love someone deeply gives you strength. Being loved by someone deeply gives you courage.

—LAO-TZU

The first duty of love is to listen.

—PAUL TILLICH

The course of true love never did run smooth.

—WILLIAM SHAKESPEARE

The way to love anything is to realize that it might be lost.

—G. K. CHESTERTON

To love another person is to see the face of God.

—VICTOR HUGO

We come to love not by finding a perfect person, but by learning to see an imperfect person perfectly.

—ANONYMOUS

We cannot really love anybody with whom we never laugh.

—AGNES REPPLIER

We seek the comfort of another. Someone to share and share the life we choose. Someone to help us through the never ending attempt to understand ourselves. And in the end, someone to comfort us along the way.

—MARLIN FINCH LUPUS

In dreams and in love there are no impossibilities.
—JANOS ARANY (1817–1882)

Love is a choice you make from moment to moment.

—BARBARA DE ANGELIS

With love and patience, nothing is impossible.
—DAISAKU IDEDA

To be capable of steady friendship or lasting love, are the two greatest proofs, not only of goodness of heart, but of strength of mind.

—PAUL AUBUCHON

This is the miracle that happens every time to those who really love; the more they give, the more they possess.

—RAINER MARIA RILKE

Grow old along with me, the best is yet to be.

—ROBERT BROWNING

I love you not only for what you are, but for what I am when I am with you.

—ELIZABETH BARRETT BROWINING

Marriages are made in heaven and consummated on Earth.

—JOHN LYLY

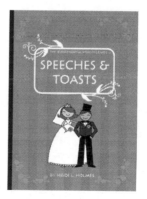

QUINTESSENTIAL WEDDING GUIDES ...
AVAILABLE FROM

blue ink designs
WWW.BLUEINKDESIGNS.COM